Run the Race

2 Timothy

by Bryson Smith

Run the Race

UK Distribution by
The Good Book Company
Elm House, 37 Elm Road
New Malden, Surrey KT3 3HB
Tel: 0845 225 0880; Fax: 0845 225 0990
email: admin@thegoodbook.co.uk
website: www.thegoodbook.co.uk

ISBN 1 876326 19 0

Cover illustration by Liz Murphy

Printed in China

Contents

	How to make the most of these studies	5
1	When the going gets tough	9
2	Protecting what's precious	13
3	Persevering in the gospel	19
4	Passing on the gospel	25
5	Helps and hindrances	33
6	Preach the gospel	41

How to make the most of these studies

1. What is an Interactive Bible Study?

These 'interactive' Bible studies are a bit like a guided tour of a famous city. The studies will take you through 2 Timothy, pointing out things along the way, filling in background details, and suggesting avenues for further exploration. But there is also time for you to do some sight-seeing of your own—to wander off, have a good look for yourself, and form your own conclusions.

In other words, we have designed these studies to fall half-way between a sermon and a set of unadorned Bible study questions. We want to provide stimulation and input and point you in the right direction, while leaving you to do a lot of the exploration and discovery yourself.

We hope that these studies will stimulate lots of 'interaction'—interaction with the Bible, with the things we've written, with your own current thoughts and attitudes, with other people as you discuss them, and with God as you talk to him about it all.

2. The format

Each study contains sections of text to introduce, summarize, suggest and provoke. We've left plenty of room in the margins for you to jot comments and questions as you read. Interspersed throughout the text are three types of 'interaction', each with their own symbol:

For starters

Questions to break the ice and get you thinking.

Investigate

Questions to help you investigate key parts of the Bible.

Think it through

Questions to help you think through the implications of your discoveries and write down your own thoughts and reactions.

When you come to one of these symbols, you'll know that it's time to do some work of your own.

3. Suggestions for Individual Study

- Before you begin, pray that God would open your eyes to what he is saying in 2 Timothy and give you the spiritual strength to do something about it. You may be spurred to pray again at the end of the study.
- Work through the study, following the directions as you go. Write in the spaces provided.
- Resist the temptation to skip over the *Think it through* sections. It is important to think about the sections of text (rather than just accepting them as true) and to ponder the implications for your life. Writing these things down is a very valuable way to get your thoughts working.
- Take what opportunities you can to talk to others about what you've learnt.

4. Suggestions for Group Study

- Much of the above applies to group study as well. The studies are suitable for structured Bible study or cell groups, as well as for more informal pairs and threesomes. Get with a friend/s and work through them at your own pace; use them as the basis for regular Bible study with your spouse. You don't need the formal structure of a 'group' to gain maximum benefit.
- It is *vital* that group members work through the study themselves *before* the group meets. The group discussion can take place comfortably in an hour (depending on how side-tracked you get!), but only if all the members have done the work and are familiar with the material.
- Spend most of the group time discussing the 'interactive' sections—*Investigate* and *Think it Through.* Reading all the text together will take too long and should be unnecessary if the group members have done their preparation. You may wish to underline and read aloud particular paragraphs or sections of text that you think are important.
- The role of the group leader is to direct the course of the discussion and to try to draw the threads together at the end. This will mean a little extra preparation—underlining important sections of text to emphasize, working out which questions are worth concentrating on, and being sure of the main thrust of the study. Leaders will also probably want to work out approximately how long they'd like to spend on each part.
- We haven't included an 'answer guide' to the questions in the studies. This is a deliberate move. We want to give you a guided tour of 2 Timothy not a lecture. There is more than enough in the text we have written and the questions we have asked to point you in what we think is the right direction. The rest is up to you.

2 Timothy 1–4

When the going gets tough

The Appalachian Trail is the longest continuous walking trail in the world. It stretches for over 3,500 km up the east coast of the United States. Walking the Appalachian Trail is virtually the equivalent of hiking from Land's End to John O'Groats three times. It's a long walk.

Each year about 2000 wide-eyed walkers try their hand at the Appalachian Trail. Very few make it. Half the walkers don't even make it one third of the way. One in ten of them drop out within the first week. There have been cases of people travelling half way around the world and spending a small fortune on camping equipment, only to pull out after three days of walking. They turn up, it would seem, expecting a nice stroll through the woods with the sun shining, birds singing and squirrels playing. What they get are rocks, mountain climbs, rain, hypothermia, ticks, bears and snakes. It just isn't what they expected.

As the saying goes, "When the going gets tough, the tough get going". When things get difficult, when things aren't as easy as you thought they might be—that's when you see a person's true colours. That's when you see what people are made of.

The going was tough for the Apostle Paul when he wrote 2 Timothy. It is a letter which shows us what Paul is made of, what his true colours are. And his colours are inspirational.

Investigate

One of the nice things about 2 Timothy is that it isn't very long. Quickly read through the following questions; then read through the whole of 2 Timothy; and then come back and answer the questions.

1. Note down as many things as you can discover about Paul's situation when he wrote the letter.

2. How many things can you discover about Timothy?

3. Why do you think Paul is writing this letter?

4. What are some words which would describe the mood of the letter? (e.g. happy, sad, angry, etc.)

5. What sorts of topics does Paul write about?

6. Are there any words or phrases which are repeated throughout the letter?

7. Did any verses stand out to you as especially powerful? Is there one particular verse which you think captures the overall message of the letter?

Guard the good deposit

As you would now appreciate after reading the letter, 2 Timothy is written at a dark time in Paul's life. He is chained up in a Roman prison (1:16-17), deserted by many (1:15, 4:16), and not expecting to live much longer (4:6-7). Against this background, he writes to Timothy to urge him to stand firm and to continue promoting the gospel. It is a stirring letter. Some of the most moving verses in the New Testament are to be found here.

For the purpose of these studies, we will be viewing 2 Timothy 1:14 as a good summary statement of the letter:

> Guard the good deposit that was entrusted to you—guard it with the help of the Holy Spirit who lives in us.

The "good deposit" is a reference to the gospel (cf 1:8ff). In other words, Paul is keen for Timothy to protect and promote the message of Jesus Christ so that when Paul himself dies, the true gospel will still be circulating.

Throughout these studies, we will discover the ways and means by which Paul wishes Timothy to guard the gospel. It's in this way that 2 Timothy has great relevance to us. The gospel is still incredibly precious and it is still worth protecting!

Throughout these studies, God's Word radically shows us just how important the gospel is, and therefore just how much trouble we ought to be prepared to go to in order to safeguard it and share it. Get ready to be instructed, rebuked, corrected, trained and changed! After all, that's what God's Word is all about (2 Tim 3:16).

Think it through

1. Imagine that you are Timothy.

    a. How would you feel after receiving a letter like 2 Timothy?

    b. What would you want to write back and tell Paul?

2. In 2 Timothy 1:14, Paul tells Timothy that "the Holy Spirit who lives in us" will help him to guard the gospel. How do you think the Spirit does this?

3. "I can't relate to the Apostle Paul. He's such a super-Christian. I only get depressed when I read his letters." How might you respond to a comment like that?

2 Timothy 1

Protecting what's precious

When something is precious, it is worth protecting. When something is special, it is worth safeguarding.

This is no better illustrated than in the extraordinary lengths to which some Hollywood celebrities go in order to protect their property and their families. The comedian Jim Carey has a house full of surveillance equipment including automated fences which spring up out of the ground at the first sign of trouble. The singer Olivia Newton-John has reportedly turned her home into a fortress, with a military-style command post in the cellar. Visitors to Madonna's home have to negotiate four separate security checkpoints, each of which is equipped with surveillance cameras and metal detectors.

If something or someone is special to you, they're worth protecting.

In our first study, we discovered that 2 Timothy is a letter written by the Apostle Paul to make sure that the gospel is protected and well-guarded. We considered 2 Timothy1:14 to be a good summary of the entire letter: *Guard the good deposit that was entrusted to you—guard it with the help of the Holy Spirit who lives in us.*

In chapter 1, Paul reminds Timothy of some of the reasons *why* the gospel is so precious that it deserves to be guarded.

Investigate

Read 2 Timothy 1

1. What has God done for us through the gospel? (vv.8-9)

2. What does it mean to be "called to a holy life"?

3. Why has God saved us? (v.9)

4. Verses 9-10 are full of wonderful ideas. Try to write each of the phrases in your own words.

   "This grace was given us in Christ Jesus before the beginning of time..."

   "...but it has now been revealed through the appearing of our Saviour, Christ Jesus..."

   "...who has destroyed death..."

   "...and has brought life and immortality to light through the gospel."

A precious gospel

The gospel is a very valuable message. It's a message of salvation *from* death *for* holiness.

Firstly, we are saved *from* death, in the sense that we no longer face death as an eternal punishment for our failures towards God. Through the gospel, we are now able to look past this earthly death to an eternal existence in heaven with God himself. Now that's an important message! A message that can lift people out of hell and put them into heaven.

But it doesn't even end there. We have not only been saved *from* death we have also been saved *for* a holy life (v.9). This is a great blessing, because the holy life is the good life. The holy life is the most rewarding and fulfilled life possible. It means not being enslaved and oppressed by the sin and false values of this world. It is life as God intended it. It's the life that works best.

The message of Jesus Christ, therefore, is no small thing. Hearing and responding to the news about Jesus lifts us out of the jaws of hell and puts us in a relationship with God in which we can now live life to the full. And all of it is by God's grace. We contribute nothing.

This gospel is astonishing—which of course is exactly what Paul is wanting Timothy to see afresh. Paul is reminding Timothy of all these things so that he'll feel the incredible value of the gospel, and therefore want to guard it and protect it.

Investigate

1. Reread chapter 1, noting down all the things which Paul says that he has done because of the gospel.

2. In verse 11, Paul mentions being a herald, an apostle and a teacher. What does each of these involve? How are they different from each other?

3. List all the things which Paul asks Timothy to do for the sake of the gospel?

4. Throughout this chapter, what verses suggest that God is actively helping both Paul and Timothy?

Extreme measures

The importance of the gospel is clearly shown by what Paul has gone through for it, and what he expects Timothy to go through for it. Paul's life has been dominated by the gospel. Now he wants Timothy's life to be dominated by it too. Paul speaks of suffering for Jesus, of being unashamed of the gospel in the face of opposition, of being a self-disciplined herald and a guardian of the gospel.

This is a good thing for us to ponder. We live in a world in which the rarer something is, the more value we place on it. But in most Western countries, we can walk into almost any book shop and buy a Bible. We can even get one for free if we know the right contacts. But we must not let the easy availability of the gospel fool us into thinking that it's not important. The gospel message is precious.

Think it through

1. What are some practical ways in which we can help each other to:

    a. Remember the value of the gospel message?

b. Pursue our calling to a holy life?

2. Paul calls on Timothy to join with him in suffering for the gospel. What are some of the ways that we might be involved in suffering for the gospel?

3. Paul also speaks in several places of not being ashamed (vv.8,12). When are we tempted to be ashamed of our faith or of other Christians?

4. What is Paul's basis for not being ashamed (v.12)? In what way is this a help to us?

5. Paul mentions Timothy's mother and grandmother as important people in Timothy's faith. Who have been important to your faith? They are precious people whom God has used. Spend some time giving thanks for them in prayer.

2 Timothy 2:1–13

Persevering in the gospel

Most of us know how to safeguard our homes. We keep them locked when we are out; perhaps we fit an alarm system; we might even have people stay in the house while we're on holidays. Most of us are pretty good at protecting our homes. But how do we safeguard the gospel? What exactly should we be doing if we want to keep safe the message of Jesus Christ?

So far, we have discovered that 2 Timothy is a letter written by the Apostle Paul asking Timothy to *safeguard the gospel* (1:14). In chapter 1, Paul reminded Timothy just how valuable the gospel is and therefore why it is necessary to safeguard it. The question now becomes: *How?*. What's involved in "guarding the good deposit"?

That's what Paul begins to explain in chapter 2.

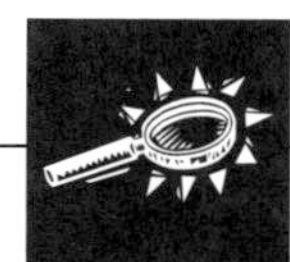

Investigate

Read 2 Timothy 2:1-2

1. What two main things does Paul ask Timothy to do in these verses?

2. What does it mean to be "strong in the grace that is in Christ Jesus"?

3. Why do you think Paul mentions the "presence of many witnesses"?

4. Given what you have answered above, try to write out verses 1-2 in your own words.

Enduring and entrusting

As chapter 2 opens, Paul points out to Timothy two important ways to "guard the good deposit". The first way is to remain loyal to it (v.1). The second way is by passing it on to other reliable people who will in turn teach others (v.2).

These two big ideas—of Timothy enduring in the gospel himself as well as entrusting the gospel to others—will dominate the rest of the chapter. In the remainder of this study we will focus on the first of these ideas. (The second idea, that of passing the gospel on to others, will be the focus of study 4.)

Investigate

Read 2 Timothy 2:3-13

1. In what sense does Paul want Timothy to be like a soldier?

2. In what sense does Paul want Timothy to be like an athlete?

3. In what sense does Paul want Timothy to be like a farmer?

4. In what ways is Paul himself a model of the things he has mentioned in verses 3-7?

5. Why do you think Paul mentions Jesus and his resurrection in verse 8? What is significant about him being “descended from David”?

6. What does it mean to die with Christ? What happens to those who do this?

7. According to verses 11-13, what will happen to people who do not remain loyal to Jesus Christ?

Enduring in the gospel

Staying strong in the gospel in the midst of a fallen world is not easy. It requires the commitment of a hard-working farmer, the self-discipline of a striving athlete, the single-mindedness of a soldier. These are characteristics which Paul himself had, and which he is encouraging Timothy to have.

But it goes further than that. In verses 11-13, Paul warns Timothy about what will happen if people don't endure with Christ. It's in this respect that verse 13 is a little unexpected. It seems to contradict the verse before it. How can God be faithful and yet disown people? It is because God will remain faithful to himself. In other words, God has promised to discipline and punish people who fall away. And he will. If we grow faithless—if we abandon the gospel and disown God—he will disown us. He has warned us, and he will do it! "He cannot disown himself."

All this leaves us with a challenge. Will we endure or are we going to fade? Have we got the commitment to keep on with Jesus even when we don't seem to be getting anything out of it? Have we got the self-discipline to be able to turn the television off or get out of bed that little bit earlier so we can spend time in personal devotion? Have we got the single-mindedness to be filling our mind with only those things which are helpful and pure? If we haven't, then we are in danger of not enduring with Jesus. And if we don't endure we certainly won't be guarding the gospel!

Think it through

1. What are some of the different reasons that people fail to endure with Jesus Christ? (compare Mark 4:16-19)

2. What are some specific ways that we can make sure that we endure?

3. What are some specific ways that we can help others to endure?

4. Spend some time praying for those brothers and sisters in Christ who are still suffering for the gospel "even to the point of being chained like a criminal".

2 Timothy 2:14–26

Passing on the gospel

We've all seen them on current affairs programs. Maybe you've even experienced them first-hand—cowboy or bogus workers who don't do the right thing for their clients. The builder who cuts corners on materials, the mechanic who uses second-hand parts but charges the customer for new parts, the 'professional' who lies about his credentials. Many people suffer distress and anxiety from poor workers such as these. The Apostle Paul is keen that no-one should suffer distress through poor workers of the gospel.

In our last study, we noted that in 2 Timothy 2:1-2 Paul explained two main ways in which Timothy could guard the gospel. Study 3 concentrated on the first of these ways—that Timothy himself stay strong in the grace of Jesus Christ. In this study, we focus on the second way of guarding the gospel, that of passing it on to reliable people who will in turn pass it on to others. And just as Paul gave three images of what it meant to persevere in the gospel (a soldier, a farmer and an athlete), he now gives another three images of what it means to effectively pass on the gospel. They are the images of a workman, a household vessel and a servant. Let's look at each of these in turn.

Gospel workmen

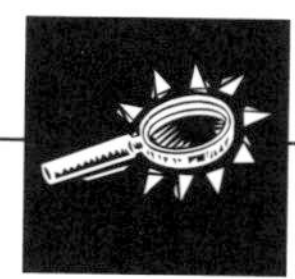

Investigate

Read 2 Timothy 2:14-20

1. Who do you think the "them" of verse 14 are?

2. What sort of workman does Paul want Timothy (and those he passes the gospel onto) to be?

3. Can you think of any examples of what "godless chatter" might be? How would this be different to "quarrelling about words" in verse 14?

4. Philetus and Hymenaeus are both examples of poor workmen. Where have they gone wrong?

5. How would you go about responding to the error that Philetus and Hymenaeus were making?

Paul has already told Timothy to entrust the gospel to "reliable men who will be qualified to teach others" (2:2). Such men need to be skilled craftsmen in how they handle the gospel, for if someone handles God's Word poorly it can do immense damage. People's eternal destiny can be ruined when teachers do a poor job of handling God's Word. That's exactly what seemed to be happening with some false teachers at the time Paul wrote to Timothy.

Because they didn't know the Scriptures well enough, they could not discern what was important and what wasn't, and so were getting into silly and trivial things.

Worse still, some had drifted from the truth altogether. Hymenaeus and Philetus claimed that the resurrection had already happened. This was bad for two reasons. Firstly, Christians would be anxious, thinking that they may have somehow missed out on the resurrection; and secondly, if the resurrection had already happened, what incentive would there be for godly living and endurance?

This is probably why Paul goes on to say that God knows who belongs to him (v.19). In other words, God won't leave any believers behind at the resurrection.

All in all, Hymenaeus and Philetus are poor workmen. And Paul says to Timothy that in order to guard the gospel he must avoid being like them and avoid entrusting the gospel to people like them. Timothy must look for reliable people who will be skilled at handling God's word.

In verses 20-22, however, Paul's imagery changes from that of a workman to that of household vessels. Let's now discover why he does this.

Gospel instruments

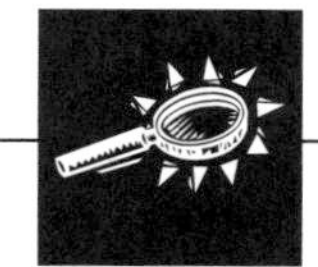

Investigate

Read 2 Timothy 2:20-22

1. What sort of articles are in a house? What are they used for?

2. How does someone become an instrument that God can use for noble purposes? What specific ways of doing this does Paul suggest for Timothy?

3. Try to think of your own words or phrases for "righteousness, faith, love and peace" (in verse 22).

4. In what ways is "an instrument for noble purposes" useful to God?

In our home, we have two types of coffee cups—the really useful mugs that we drink from all the time, and the fine china ones with silly little handles that you can't get your fingers through. We don't use this second sort very much at all.

In God's household, he wants us to be vessels that he can use all the time. In verse 21, God tells us that the way to be useful is to cleanse ourselves—in other words, to be godly.

This is a very important point. For a teacher to effectively pass on the gospel, they must not only handle the gospel well, they must also live a godly life. The two things go together. Indeed, so important is the aspect of holiness that Paul continues to emphasize it with another image, this time of a servant.

Gospel servants

Investigate

Read 2 Timothy 2:23-26

1. Verse 24 speaks of "the Lord's servant". What images does the word 'servant' conjure up?

2. What things must the Lord's servant avoid?

3. What are some of the ways that they should avoid these things?

4. These verses focus on arguments and disagreements. What responsibilities do each of the following have in disagreements?
   - God
   - the Lord's servant
   - the other person in the disagreement

In the closing verses of this chapter, Paul explains to Timothy that an effective teacher of God's Word must be a gentle servant at times of disagreement. Rather than argue in a heated or hostile way, God's servant should explain the truth in love. God's servant doesn't wish to win an argument simply to protect his or her ego; rather he or she simply wishes to be as clear as possible, so that God might bring conviction through his Word.

In this study, we have built up a challenging list of criteria for teachers of God's Word. In order to be reliable and effective teachers who pass on the gospel, they must be skilled craftsmen at handling the Word (2:14-19); they must be godly examples of the Word (2:20-22); and they must be humble and gentle instructors in the Word (2:23-26). These are high standards indeed. But what could be more worthy of such standards than the precious gospel of Jesus Christ?

Think it through

1. Pointless arguments and quarrelling have been referred to several times in these verses. What modern day examples can you think of? What are some practical steps that we can take to not be drawn into such disputes?

2. Are there ever times when it is necessary to quarrel?

3. What is actually involved in correctly handling the word of truth (v.15)? Suggest ways that we can equip ourselves for this task.

4. Do you think the "evil desires of youth" are any different to the evil desires of middle age or even old age?

5. What does 2 Timothy 2:14-26 have to say about how we should treat our church leaders, and what we should expect from them?

6. Can you think of specific godly teachers who have gently instructed you in God's Word? Spend some time thanking God for them.

2 Timothy 3

Helps and hindrances

I love watching the 4 x 100m relays at the Olympic Games. I enjoy the excitement of watching the runners work together to get the baton around the track. Of course, there are two aspects to a relay that must both work well if the relay is to be successful. First, each member of the team must run their race to the end. If they pull a muscle, if they give up out of tiredness, if they run out of their lane, the relay breaks down. Each runner must endure. But the relay can also break down if each runner doesn't successfully hand over the baton. There's no point running a personal best if you then don't give the baton to the next runner. It's a relay—the baton must be passed on!

In our last two studies, we have listened to Paul explaining to Timothy that he is in a gospel relay. And like any relay, Timothy must not only persevere (study 3), he must work to pass the gospel baton on to others (study 4). Persevering *and* passing on—both have to happen if Timothy is to guard the gospel effectively.

In 2 Timothy 3, Paul continues to speak to Timothy about things which will influence the effectiveness of the gospel relay. The chapter falls into two main sections. In the first section (vv.1-9), Paul describes things in the world which act to hinder the gospel relay. In the second section (vv.10-16), Paul describes things which he has done and which Timothy must do in order to help the gospel relay. Let's deal with each section in turn.

Hindrances

Investigate

Read 2 Timothy 3:1-9

1. When are the last days? Does Paul think that Timothy is experiencing them? (look also at Jude 17-19)

2. Does the term “people” mentioned in verse 2 refer to everyone, or does Paul have specific people in mind? What implications does our answer have for the second half of verse 5? (You might also compare 1 Cor 5:9-11.)

3. What does it mean to have “a form of godliness but denying its power” in verse 5?

4. Of the characteristics mentioned in verses 1-5, which, if any, of them are commonly regarded as virtues in our modern world?

5. How do the characteristics listed in verses 2-5 specifically express themselves in the false teachers in verses 6-9?

6. How is it that people as terrible as those mentioned in verses 1-5 could possibly gain control over the women of verse 6?

7. Jannes and Jambres (v.8) are thought to be two of the Egyptian magicians who opposed Moses. Read what happened in Exodus 7:10-13. In what ways are the false teachers similar to Jannes and Jambres?

We live in a fallen world which loves to love the wrong things in life (notice how many times love is mentioned in vv.2-4). Rather than loving God, their Creator, the people of this world choose instead to love aspects of his creation. Because of this, people are given over to self-absorbed, self-gratifying desires, pursuits and pastimes.

Sadly the church is not immune from such people. In particular, Paul has his sights on some especially despicable characters who are using secretive and deceptive methods to gain control over "weak-willed women". For these false teachers, life is all about making themselves happy, comfortable, entertained, fulfilled, secure, titillated and highly thought of. Worse still, all of this comes under the guise of respectability (v.5).

Such people are a scandalous hindrance to the gospel of Jesus Christ. They are like saboteurs who grease the baton in the relay, or try to trip the runners, or get in the way of the change-over. They drag the gospel into disrepute as they drag others away from it. They are nothing like the gentle, godly servants whom Paul has described in the previous chapter (2:22-26). Paul wants Timothy to be very different—which is exactly what he goes on to say.

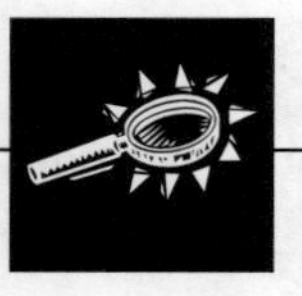

Helps

Investigate

Read 2 Timothy 3:10-16

1. What sort of life has Paul had?

2. How is this different from the life of the false teachers?

3. What sort of teaching methods does Paul want Timothy to pursue? How is this different from the false teachers?

4. What does it mean for Scripture to be "God-breathed"?

5. What difference—if any—is there between teaching, rebuking, correcting and training?

Having described the godless ways of the last days, Paul now turns to describe the godliness he expects from Timothy. Timothy is to model himself on Paul. Whereas the false teachers were characterized by selfishness, Paul is characterized by selflessness. So selfless is Paul that for the sake of the gospel he has been prepared to work long hours, make sacrifices, get tired, be arrested, endure shipwrecks, face ridicule, deal with confrontation and be assaulted.

The way of the world is to be lovers of self, which means chasing after pleasure. Timothy is to be a lover of God, and that means putting up with persecutions.

But it is not just in character that Timothy is to be different. It is also in method. As we've seen, the false teachers were secretive manipulators. By contrast, Timothy's method was to be the simple, straightforward teaching of Scripture—because the Scripture is all that is needed to equip us for every good work (v.16).

Here, then, are important lessons to help Timothy guard the gospel. He is to be different from the world. He is to love God more than himself. He is to use God's Word clearly and faithfully. If we also wish to guard the gospel, these are powerful lessons for us as well.

Think it through

1. Do you think Paul's warnings about false teachers to Timothy are still relevant today? Why/why not?

2. How can we protect ourselves against false teachers?

3. Paul says that "everyone who wants to live a godly life in Christ Jesus will be persecuted". What types of persecution are you experiencing?

4. If someone isn't experiencing much persecution, does this mean that they aren't serious enough about being godly?

5. If Scripture is God-breathed, what should be our attitude towards it?

6. Given what Paul says about Scripture in verses 16-17, what role is there for the following:

- Christian books other than the Bible

- Christian music

- other Christians

2 Timothy 4

Preach the gospel

A friend once told me of a school boy who was a very good football player—so good, in fact, that several of his games were watched by big-time talent scouts. The interesting thing about the talent scouts was that they paid very little attention to what happened in the early part of the game. Sometimes they didn't even arrive until mid-way through the second half. The talent scouts knew that everyone comes out with a full head of steam in the first few minutes of a game. During those opening moments, all the players are enthusiastic, energetic and intense. But the talent scouts weren't interested in the start. They were interested in the finish. They wanted to see who was still running and tackling in the last few minutes. The mark of a good player is not how they start but how they finish.

Being a Christian isn't much different. Lots of people start out following Jesus with great enthusiasm. They do lots of good things; they say lots of good things. But in the end, it matters very little how you start. It's how you finish that counts.

How do you think you're going to finish? How would you like to finish?

For the sake of the gospel, the Apostle Paul wants Timothy to finish strongly. In fact, that's why he wrote the letter we call 2 Timothy. We've seen over the last five studies that this letter was written at a time when many people were *not* finishing well. People were deserting Paul and the gospel in large numbers. Everything Paul had been working for seemed to be falling apart. He was in prison not expecting to come out alive. His friends and former colleagues were leaving him like rats from a sinking ship. Worse still, they were falling away from the gospel.

Here in the final chapter of this letter, in some of the most moving verses of the New Testament, Paul gathers his thoughts for one last, emotional plea for Timothy to finish well.

Investigate

Read 2 Timothy 4:1-8

1. Why do you think Paul starts this section in such a dramatic way?

2. What does Paul want Timothy to do and how does Paul want him to do it?

3. Why do you think Paul is so focussed on wanting Timothy to preach the Word? (look back at 3:16)

4. What does it mean to be prepared "in season and out of season"?

5. In what ways does Paul want Timothy to be different from many other teachers?

6. What sorts of things do you think "itching ears like to hear"?

7. Try and write verses 6-8 in your own words.

v.6

v.7

v.8

The good fight

Three words dominate this closing chapter: "Preach the Word". At the time Paul wrote this letter, a lot of people who were meant to be doing this weren't doing it. In our last study, we read about scheming, manipulative people who were influencing and leading others away from the truth. In these verses, we discover weak and selfish teachers who only say things to ingratiate themselves to their audiences.

Paul concludes his letter by urging Timothy not to be like them. It is the Bible that thoroughly equips people for every good work. It is the Bible that trains us in righteousness. So it is the Bible that Timothy should teach. Only when the Bible is taught faithfully, clearly and boldly will the gospel be effectively protected and promoted.

Paul for his part has done exactly what he expects Timothy to do. And because Paul has endured with Christ, he will also reign with Christ (2:12).

Investigate

Read 2 Timothy 4:9-22

1. What hardships has Paul experienced?

2. In the midst of these hardships:

   a. What encouragements does Paul mention?

   b. How does Paul feel about God?

3. What do you think Paul means in verse 18 when he says, "The Lord will rescue me from every evil attack"?

The central importance of the gospel

As we finish these studies on 2 Timothy, we are left with an inspiring picture of a man who understood the importance of the gospel. Paul knows that he is about to die. He is not running the race anymore—he has finished the race. And what a way to finish! Paul's consuming passion is for Christ to be honoured by the spreading of the gospel. Everything Paul does, everything he thinks, every decision he makes—it's all about the gospel being promoted. Here he is, virtually writing from his death bed and what is he concerned for? That the Word be preached. That the gospel be guarded.

A survey was taken in the United States of people 95 years and over, asking them what they would change if they could have their lives over again. If they had a second chance what would they do differently? Their top three answers were:

- they would have taken more time to reflect about life rather than simply reacting to it;
- they would have liked to have taken more risks; and
- they would have liked to have done more things which would have outlived them.

Had he lived to the age of 95, the Apostle Paul would not have given any of those answers. Through the grace of God, Paul had reflected on life deeply. He had certainly taken some risks. And he had worked for a Kingdom that would last forever.

Such is the privilege of protecting and promoting the gospel of our Lord Jesus Christ.

Think it through

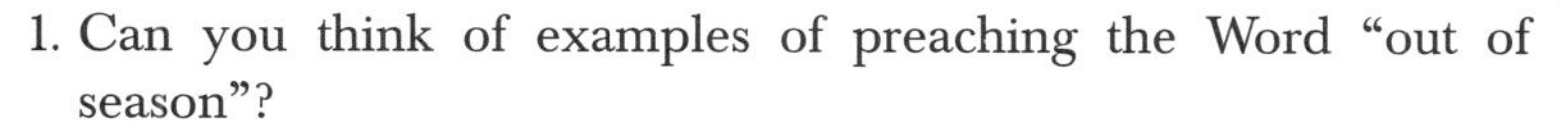

1. Can you think of examples of preaching the Word "out of season"?

2. Why do you think it is that people "will not put up with sound doctrine"?

3. What different ways can we equip ourselves for the task of sharing the Word with people?

4. What do you need to do to ensure that you keep the faith and finish the race?

5. Quickly skim back through 2 Timothy. Have there been any issues over which you have been corrected, rebuked or encouraged?

6. How are you going to change your life as a result of studying 2 Timothy?

Who are we?

Ever since we opened our doors in 1991 in the UK as St Matthias Press, our aim has been to provide the Christian community with products of a uniformly high standard–both in their biblical faithfulness and in the quality of the writing and production.

Now known asThe Good Book Company, we have grown to become an international provider of user-friendly resources, with Christians of all sorts using our Bible studies, books, Briefings, audio cassettes, videos, training courses and events.

Buy direct from us and save

If you order your resources direct from us, you can not only save time and money, you invest in more great resources for the future:

- you save time–we usually despatch our orders within 24 hours of receiving them
- you save money–if you order in bulk, you'll save even more
- you help keep us afloat–because we get more from each sale, buying from us direct helps us to stay alive and develop new Biblical resources for the future.

Please call us for a free catalogue of all our resources, including an up-to-date list of other titles in this Interactive Bible Studies series. Some details of IBS titles are contained on the following page.

Email: admin@thegoodbook.co.uk
Website: www.thegoodbook.co.uk

Interactive Bible studies

Our Interactive Bible studies (IBS) and Topical Bible Studies (TBS) are a valuable resource to help you keep feeding from God's Word. The IBS series works through passages and books of the Bible; the TBS series pulls together the Bible's teaching on topics, such as money or prayer. As of January 2004, the series contains the following 30 titles. Call us or visit the website for the most up-to-date listing. 0845 225 0880; www.thegoodbook.co.uk

OLD TESTAMENT

FULL OF PROMISE (THE BIG PICTURE OF THE O.T.)
Authors: Phil Campbell & Bryson Smith, 8 studies

BEYOND EDEN (GENESIS 1-11)
Authors: Phillip Jensen and Tony Payne, 9 studies

THE ONE AND ONLY (DEUT)
Author: Bryson Smith, 8 studies

THE GOOD, THE BAD & THE UGLY (JUDGES)
Author: Mark Baddeley, 10 studies

FAMINE & FORTUNE (RUTH)
Authors: Barry Webb & David Hohne, 4 studies

THE EYE OF THE STORM (JOB)
Author: Bryson Smith, 6 studies

THE SEARCH FOR MEANING (ECCLESIASTES)
Author: Tim McMahon, 9 studies

TWO CITIES (ISAIAH)
Authors: Andrew Reid and Karen Morris, 9 studies

KINGDOM OF DREAMS (DANIEL)
Authors: Andrew Reid and Karen Morris, 8 studies

RENOVATOR'S DREAM (NEH)
Phil Campbell & Greg Clarke, 7 studies

WARNING SIGNS (JONAH)
Author: Andrew Reid, 6 studies

BURNING DESIRE (OBADIAH & MALACHI)
Authors: Phillip Jensen and Richard Pulley, 6 studies

NEW TESTAMENT

THE GOOD LIVING GUIDE (MATTHEW 5:1-12)
Authors: Phillip Jensen and Tony Payne, 9 studies

NEWS OF THE HOUR (MARK)
Author: Peter Bolt, 10 studies

FREE FOR ALL (GALATIANS)
Authors: Phillip Jensen & Kel Richards, 8 studies

WALK THIS WAY (EPHESIANS)
Author: Bryson Smith, 8 studies

PARTNERS FOR LIFE (PHILIPPIANS)
Author: Tim Thorburn, 8 studies

THE COMPLETE CHRISTIAN (COLOSSIANS)
Authors: Phillip Jensen and Tony Payne, 8 studies

ALL LIFE IS HERE (1 TIMOTHY)
Authors: Phillip Jensen and Greg Clarke, 9 studies

RUN THE RACE (2 TIMOTHY)
Author: Bryson Smith, 6 studies

THE PATH TO GODLINESS (TITUS)
Authors: Phillip Jensen an
Tony Payne, 6 studies

FROM SHADOW TO REALITY (HEBREWS)
Author: Joshua Ng, 10 studie

THE IMPLANTED WORD (JAM
Authors: Phillip Jensen an
K.R. Birkett, 8 studies

HOMEWARD BOUND (1 PETER)
Authors: Phillip Jensen an
Tony Payne, 10 studies

ALL YOU NEED TO KNOW (2 PETER)
Author: Bryson Smith, 6 studies

THE VISION STATEMENT (REVELATION)
Author: Greg Clarke, 9 studi

TOPICAL BIBLE STUDIES

BOLD I APPROACH (PRAYER)
Author: Tony Payne, 6 studies

CASH VALUES (MONEY)
Author: Tony Payne, 5 studies

THE BLUEPRINT (DOCTRINE)
Authors: Phillip Jensen & Tony Payne, 11 studies

WOMAN OF GOD (THE BIBLE ON WOMEN)
Author: Terry Blowes, 8 stuc